How to Take the
Bible to Work

Woodrow Kroll

BACK TO THE BIBLE
LINCOLN, NE 68501

17000 printed to date—1995
(1150-220—4M—55)
ISBN 0-8474-0893-0

Unless otherwise noted, all Scripture quotations are from
The New King James Version.

Printed in the United States of America.

Introduction

God ordained the local church to evangelize the world and to equip the saints for meaningful service to Him. The Lord Jesus wants us to be convinced that He is the Christ, the Son of the living God, and to communicate that belief to others (Matt. 16:13-17; 28:19–20).

Does that mean your local church is the only place you learn about Jesus? Does it mean you communicate your beliefs only in church? Not at all. We go to church to worship, to sing and to praise the Lord. We go to hear the Word expounded and explained. We go to have our spiritual batteries recharged and be challenged to serve the Savior.

But if we do that just once or twice a week and what we glean from inside the church doesn't change the way we live outside of it, we have failed to grasp why God established His Church.

In some respects, the church is a staging area for an army. We get our marching orders there; we prepare ourselves for battle there; we commune with our Commander-in-Chief there. But we don't fight there—at least we shouldn't!

Jesus sent His disciples to do battle in the world, not in the church. "Go therefore and make disciples of all the nations" (Matt. 28:19). Our work as believers lies predominantly outside the church. We live in a working world, and that's where we both evangelize and grow in the grace and knowledge of our Lord and Savior Jesus Christ (2 Pet. 3:18). Once we grasp this truth, it will change how we view our work.

Chapter 1

Why Go to Work?

Have you given much thought to why you work? For most of us there is an obvious answer: to earn a living. Ask any of your friends why they go to work, and they'll say something like, "I work so I can maintain my chosen lifestyle." A more philosophical person may say, "I work because it gives my life meaning; it defines who I am and gives me self-esteem."

Some people work because they have to. They have a work ethic that will not let them do nothing. Robert Frost said, "The world is full of willing people; some willing to work, the rest willing to let them."

Maybe you're a part of the third group—willing to work because you have been taught to work hard. And while we all should be willing, even eager, to work hard, God never intended for us to work for any of these reasons.

In this chapter I want to introduce to you the biblical reason for going to work each day. It's a reason you may not immediately think of, and unsaved people would never think of, but it's God's reason and therefore should be ours as well.

I'm indebted to my friends at the Christian Business Men's Committee and their booklet *Why Go to*

Work? (Vision Foundation, Inc.). This booklet is part of their "Ministry in the Marketplace" series and more fully addresses this subject than I do here.

God gave us work for good

I believe God's account of how the world came into being. The Bible says, "In the beginning God created the heavens and the earth" (Gen. 1:1). The theory of evolution notwithstanding, God is more likely than man to know what happened before man arrived on the scene.

If we take the Genesis account of creation seriously, we must also take seriously what God said about His creation. After God finished six days of creation, Genesis 1:31 says, "Then God saw everything that He had made, and indeed it was very good." That means all things that existed before man's fall were good.

For example, the earth was an idyllic place before it was ruined by man's sin. The streams were pure and unpolluted. The air was fresh and clean. The garden God planted in Eden was breathtakingly beautiful. Adam was a good warden of this earth. Even before the fall, God "put him in the garden of Eden to tend and keep it" (Gen. 2:15).

"Free men freely work: Whoever fears God, fears to set at ease." — Elizabeth Barrett Browning

---

Since work preceded sin and the fall of man, and since it was God's desire that Adam work, we can only conclude that work is good, because everything before the fall was good. Work did not come as a result of the curse. Work isn't a curse; it's a blessing.

Theodore Roosevelt said, "No man needs sympathy because he has to work, because he has a burden to carry. Far and away the best prize that life offers is the chance to work hard at work worth doing."

God gave us work as a gift

But God did not dictate work for our good; He *gave* it to us for our good. Work is not only good, it is God's gift to us.

You may think the job you have is just dull drudgery, and maybe your work is dull. But to think about taking the Bible to work, you must see your work as a gift from God.

One of the great themes of Ecclesiastes is the vanity of everything we do that is not done for eternity—including our work. But another great theme of that book is the enjoyment of our work because it is the gift of God.

"There is nothing better for a man than that he should eat and drink, and that his soul should enjoy good in his labor. This also, I saw, was from the hand of God" (Eccl. 2:24).

"I know that there is nothing better for them than . . . that every man should eat and drink and enjoy the good of all his labor—it is the gift of God" (3:12–13).

"It is good and fitting for one to eat and drink, and to enjoy the good of all his labor . . . which God gives him; for it is his heritage. As for every man to whom God has given riches and wealth, and given him power to eat of it, to receive his heritage and rejoice in his labor—this is the gift of God" (Eccl. 5:18–19).

God gave us work for our good. He gave it as a gift. But God did not give us work simply to make money, to earn a living or to provide for our family. He has a more profound plan for our work.

God gave us work as a platform

When Jesus taught His Sermon on the Mount, He included words about work and worry. He commanded, "Therefore do not worry, saying, 'What shall we eat?' or 'What shall we drink?' or 'What shall we wear?'" (Matt. 6:31). These are the worries that drive most people to work. But Jesus had a better idea.

While God uses our work to supply our needs, He does not want us to go to work worrying about those needs. If God takes care of the lilies of the field (vv. 28–29), He'll take care of us. The bottom line? Work is not about food, clothing or shelter. Work is about doing what God saved us to do. "For we are His workmanship, created in Christ Jesus for good works, which God prepared beforehand that we should walk in them" (Eph. 2:10).

The things we go to work to gain, the things we worry about, are provided by God when we go to work to seek the first His kingdom and His righteousness (Matt. 6:33).

When we see our work as a platform for service to God instead of a place to make money, we will view why God sends us to the office or the factory or the store in a different light. He sends us there not to make money but to be His witnesses.

Some may argue that the people they minister to are different from the people they work with. They may say that they don't want to mix the secular and the sacred. They work for their employer, and they don't want to ruin their testimony by seeking the kingdom of God at their secular place of employment.

God doesn't compartmentalize our lives, and neither should we. We are not employees nine to five and Christians the rest of the time. We spend too much of our lives on the job to factor Christ out of our employment.

You can be a witness for the Lord on your job, even if it's only at break time or lunch time. You can enjoy a Bible study with others at work, if you know how to do it and you do it without cheating your employer.

Since you spend approximately one-third of your life at work, don't you think it's time to set aside your worries about what you will eat or what you will wear and begin to think about what you will say to the Lord Jesus at the Judgment Seat of Christ about how you used that part of your life?

Think about it. God made work for our good. He gave work to us as a gift. But it wasn't a gift to make money alone. It was the gift to be a platform to serve Him.

In the chapters that follow we focus on how to start a Bible study at your workplace. It's a great way to seek the kingdom of God where you spend so much of your life.

Chapter 2

Make the Right Preparations

If you are to succeed in sponsoring a Bible study at work, you must think it through before you ask your boss for permission. Be prepared to answer any question and allay any fear. Here are some essential preparations you must make.

Pray, pray, pray

Often we fail in a new ministry because we do not ask God for His help and direction. "You do not have because you do not ask. You ask and do not receive, because you ask amiss" (James 4:2–3). Before you do anything, pray.

Someone said there are four steps to accomplishment: Plan purposefully. Prepare prayerfully. Proceed positively. Pursue persistently. That's good advice for you. Plan purposefully, but don't forget to prepare prayerfully.

Get others to join you in prayer. Tell your Sunday school class and your pastor. Ask every Christian you know to pray that God will bless your workplace Bible study. There is power in corporate prayer. That's why the early church prayed together so frequently (Acts 1:14; 3:1; 6:4; 12:5; 16:13,16). They knew

God would hear their prayers singly, but they also knew God delights when His people pray in concert.

What will you pray for? First, pray that your boss will be open to the idea. Pray that he or she will see a Bible study as a way of strengthening the moral fiber of the employees. If you plan to meet with your coworkers at another location, pray that those who oversee that place will be amenable to the idea.

Ask God to open the hearts of those around you at work. Pray that your Bible study will get off to a good start and experience steady growth. Pray that the idea will catch on and minister to many.

But more than anything else, pray that God will use your workplace Bible study to lead your coworkers to know and trust in Christ as their Savior. It's a mistake to think that only believers are interested in Bible study. In fact, some who get no teaching in a local church are actually eager to know what God thinks about things. Pray that God will save the unbelievers in your group and that all of your group will grow in the grace and knowledge of our Lord and Savior Jesus Christ (2 Pet. 3:18).

Choose an appropriate launch date

When you begin your workplace Bible study may determine whether it succeeds or not. Ask God for wisdom in your choice of a launch date.

January is a good time to begin a Bible study. Many people are attuned to spiritual matters at the beginning of the year. Some are thinking about renewal. Others have made New Year's resolutions that you can help them fulfill.

September is an equally good choice. There's a fresh spirit in the early fall as students return to school, sports teams kick off new seasons, and television networks tout their new lineups. People are thinking about beginning a new cycle, so it's a good time to introduce a new activity.

Avoid starting your Bible study in the summer. Attendance would be erratic, as people are vacationing or involved in so many other activities.

"By failing to prepare, you are preparing to fail." — Benjamin Franklin

---

Just as important as the month you begin is the day you begin. You may have no control over what day of the week you will meet, but if you do, don't make it Monday. For many employees, that day is a downer. Plus, in the United States we celebrate many holidays on Monday, regardless of when they fall on the calendar. If you meet on Monday, you will miss a number of meeting days each year due to holidays.

Friday may not be a good day either. Working people have their minds elsewhere on Friday, and they are rushing around to complete work before the weekend.

Secure a popular meeting place

Hold your Bible study in a reliable, convenient and popular place. Don't choose an out-of-the-way place. You're not entering a monastery; you're conducting a

Bible study that you pray will attract more and more of your friends. Make it a visible place.

Jesus taught in the temple daily (Matt. 21:23; 26:55). It was the most public place in all Israel. Don't shun the most public place in your office building or factory.

Conference rooms make good Bible study classrooms. So do alcoves in the lunchroom or private dining rooms. They are public places that allow for some privacy. You don't want a room where people are passing through like trains on the Long Island Railroad. It should be public in the sense of being visible, but private in the sense of being quiet.

Perhaps your Bible study group will not be permitted to meet at your workplace. Maybe there's even a better place to meet. Lots of Bible studies are conducted in restaurants. Some restaurants and hotels will provide a meeting room for just the price of your meals. You can fellowship over the meal and then remain for serious study in the Word. This is an attractive way to invite new people to your Bible study.

When choosing a popular meeting place, plan for expansion. You don't want a change of venue too often, so make sure the place you choose is adequate for growth. Expect God's blessing; plan for it.

Get the word out

The final step in preparation is to publicize the Bible study. You don't want this to be a completely private study of the Word! You want as many as possible to benefit from seeking the kingdom of God at work. That means you have to get the word out.

Start by asking permission of your employer. Tell him or her exactly what you hope to accomplish with the Bible study. Lay it all out. That way you don't have to fear any misunderstanding with your employer. Ask permission to advertise with the most effective form possible. Show him your plan; get his permission. In this way, you'll keep a good relationship with your boss.

Then, do whatever you can to publicize your meeting. If you can put up posters in the cafeteria, do that. If you can print fliers to hand out to employees, do that.

A nice touch is to print personal invitation cards if you work in a small office or company. Your coworkers will feel important enough to you to have received a special invitation.

If your company or office has a newsletter, ask permission to put an announcement in it. Make it brief and interesting. Use E-mail and computer bulletin boards, if they are accessible. And of course, invite people personally, face-to face—the best way yet.

Whatever form of publicity you choose, begin to advertise weeks in advance. Then, plan for a special first day of your Bible study—one that no one will want to miss. If your coworkers see that you are serious about your Bible study and they return each week, it will become an important contribution to life at work.

Chapter 3

Present the Right Study

When you have secured permission for your workplace Bible study and have promoted it, the first day will arrive with excitement, anticipation and not a little apprehension. What will you do? What study in God's Word will you present?

Much of your success in holding and building a study group will depend on choosing the right study. Here are some tips on what to choose.

Choose an entry-level study

Don't assume that people who do not attend church know nothing of the Bible. And don't assume that people who attend church know everything about it. Neither is true.

It's important you choose an entry-level study that will satisfy both the person who has been a Christian for years and the person who has never heard John 3:16. A good way to do that is to begin with one of the four gospels—perhaps John or Luke.

John and Luke wrote their gospels in ways that are both understandable and challenging—understandable for the novice student and challenging for the old pro. These gospels record the life of Jesus, who

He is, His miracles and His teachings and, most importantly, explain how to go to heaven. The Gospel of John or the Gospel of Luke is a good entry-level study for your workplace group.

Also good are the historical books. The Book of Acts is easy to understand, tells how the church grew rapidly in the first century, features the conversion stories of notable people and contains the Gospel. Many people enjoy history, which makes Acts a good entry-level study.

Don't neglect the Old Testament. The historical books of Joshua and Judges or 1 and 2 Samuel are also interesting. They could be your first foray into the Old Testament after you finish an entry-level study in the New Testament.

Variety will make your Bible study interesting, so don't spend months on the same book or topic. Vary the topics you teach to your study group. Mix it up between Old Testament and New, between book and topical studies. Even throw in some simple theological studies as you go along.

"Well begun, half done" is an old but true maxim. Half the battle in keeping your coworkers interested in your study is to start off with a bang, so plan an entry-level study that will be enjoyable and beneficial.

Invite interaction

Psychologist Carl Jung said that the meeting of two personalities is like the contact of two chemical substances; if there is any reaction, both are transformed.

Interaction not only adds interest to your study; it provides a certain chemistry that enables everyone to be a part of the learning process. But be careful. You must set the parameters of interaction, lest your chemistry become alchemy.

Don't allow one person to dominate the interaction. (There will always be someone who tries!) You can diffuse that tendency by speaking to that person privately or by saying, "Thanks for your comment. Let's have some of the rest of you tell us what you think."

Interaction is good, but it should not dominate your teaching time. If it does, little teaching will take place. Limit interaction during your teaching so you can have a question-and-answer session at the end. This will give you ample opportunity to teach the Word and others a chance to respond to it.

Affirm the value of your group's questions. There are no dumb questions, only dumb answers. Perhaps the question one person asks is the same one others wanted to ask but were too shy. Make sure the atmosphere does not inhibit questions, especially at the close of the study.

No matter how informal the setting, some people still are timid about asking questions. They want answers, but they don't want to identify themselves as the questioner. So invite the group to hand in unsigned questions on 3 x 5 cards. That way you can interact with the questioner without identifying who it is.

Interaction is important to learning. If your Bible study becomes a lecture, interest may wane.

Be informal

Another key to conducting a "user-friendly" Bible study group is to be informal. There are no big shots in a study group; there are only fellow pilgrims on the road to spiritual maturity.

In the book *A Severe Mercy*, C. S. Lewis wrote, "Think of me as a fellow-patient in the same hospital who, having been admitted a little earlier, could give some advice." That's what you are as the teacher of your Bible study group. You may be a master teacher, but you should act like a fellow-learner.

Be informal. Walk around as you teach and interact with the group. Get close to your fellow-learners. Show them you are one of them. Use first names, even nicknames, to enhance the spirit of camaraderie. Make learning fun for everyone. People learn more in a non-threatening setting than they do in any other.

It's important in a workplace Bible study that you keep the subject matter simple and understandable. Avoid controversial issues. Your purpose is not to settle the deeper theological issues but to help bring your colleagues to Christ and help them grow in their faith.

Use visuals often

Visuals are always an aid to learning. Use your ingenuity to bring "show and tell" to your study group. These are always fun and enhance the learning process.

Once in our Back to the Bible chapel I was explaining our philosophy of a family of ministries, which in part is to use as many media as possible to proclaim the Gospel. We use radio, literature, video, computers and more to teach the Word and touch the world.

To help our staff appreciate this, I brought coffee and a coffee brewer to chapel, along with a picture of brewing coffee and a white board. As I began to speak I wrote the word *coffee* on the white board without any explanation. Minutes later I held up the picture of brewing coffee.

As the chapel progressed I put a couple of scoops of coffee in the coffee maker and poured water into it. In a few minutes we all saw the coffee dripping into the coffee pot. We saw the steam and smelled the aroma. Finally, I poured a cup of coffee for myself and offered a cup to others.

My point was clear. The word *coffee* gives you a mental image of what it is, but that image is not as deep as when you see a picture of a steaming cup of coffee. Your image is deepened when you see it brewing, smell the aroma and hear it dripping into the coffee pot. Drinking the coffee is the final step in deepening the impression.

When we use a variety of media to teach the Word, we deepen the impression on those around us. My visual enabled me to communicate that message. So will yours, so use a visual whenever possible.

Give a discreet invitation

Workplace Bible studies are God-given opportunities for evangelism; don't lose those opportunities. When you present a study that contains the Gospel—and that should be often—always provide an opportunity for those in the group to respond.

An invitation to receive Jesus as Savior isn't limited to singing "Just As I Am" and a call to walk down the aisle. There is a place for this type of invitation, but your Bible study is not that place.

There are many ways to give a discreet invitation. They are effective, they accomplish the same goal as a church invitation, and they do it without embarrassing those with whom you work. Here are some suggestions.

When you give an invitation to consider the claims of Christ, ask everyone to bow their heads. This makes their decision private, between God and them. Invite them to indicate their desire to talk with you about salvation by opening their eyes and catching your eye or by raising their hand. That way you know whom to approach after the meeting has finished.

"The world has more winnable people than ever before." — Donald McGavran

---

If someone does linger after the study, ask him discreetly if he is there to talk with you about salvation. Then take him to a distant corner or into another room and talk with him privately.

Be creative. Your ultimate goal is to talk with a friend about his need for salvation. Change the form of your invitation frequently, but always have a response device that a person can complete and leave behind. When the Spirit of God has brought a person to a point of commitment so that he has put his need in writing, you have a hard contact for follow-up evangelism.

Whatever you do, don't let the opportunity for evangelism slip through your fingers. If you present the right study, the Spirit of God will do the rest. Be ready for His results.

Chapter 4

Provide the Right Follow-up

Beginning a workplace Bible study is a worthy endeavor. It's not easy to begin, but even more difficult is continuing and thriving. Harder yet is building for the future. Unless you want your Bible study to be like the grass that takes quick root, flourishes a short time and then fades without lasting consequence, providing the right follow-up is crucial.

You provide the right follow-up when you know and appreciate the needs of your group, the local church and your employer and your own needs. Let's explore what the right follow-up means for all these needs.

Be available for discipleship and counseling

Your Bible study group may meet for an hour a week. That's minimal time—time only to plant a seed and spark interest. Therefore, you must make room for discipleship and counseling apart from your group's meeting time. That's when the real teaching takes place.

What must you remember about follow-up discipleship? First, don't do it on company time. That would be a violation of your employer's graciousness in permitting a workplace study. Set a time for follow-up discipleship on your time.

There may be exceptions to this rule. Perhaps your work situation is such that you have hours of downtime as you wait for someone else to do his job first. If that's the case, you may be able to use that time in personal discipleship. Touch base with your employer first; don't do anything secretively.

Be biblical when you counsel your work colleagues. You used the Bible to teach them; there's no reason not to use it to counsel and disciple them. Scripture has answers to spiritual questions. If you can't find an answer, ask your pastor or some other mature believer to help you. Personal discipleship not only helps your friend grow in the Lord, it helps you grow too.

Keep some discipleship materials on hand. These can range from tracts to booklets to personal Bible study courses. Check with your church library, your pastor or a local Christian bookstore or Bible college about what resources are available for discipleship. There are many.

Campus Crusade, the Navigators and Back to the Bible are just some of the Christian ministries that provide discipleship materials. Know what is available and get some before you begin your study.

What should you do when you get in over your head? When the one you are discipling has questions you can't answer? When the counsel he needs is of a more technical nature than you can provide?

Admit when you have reached the limit of your counsel, and match your colleague with someone who can help him. If he needs pastoral counsel, ask your pastor for an appointment. If he needs other kinds of help, ask your pastor to suggest other professionals to you.

Don't do what you are not qualified to do. As a student of the Word, you can significantly help your colleagues; but when you can't, seek the help of those who can. After all, helping your friend is what matters, not who provides the help.

Build a group that outlives you

Providing the right follow-up also means that you build a Bible study group that will outlive your involvement with it. This requires maturity on your part, but it is the true measure of success.

You need to invest yourself in the lives of other teachers for your group. Begin right away to identify and train some Joshuas and Timothys. Build a list of substitute teachers and use them wisely.

Perhaps you have someone in the group with a particular interest or expertise in a special Bible topic. Invite him to teach a month of special studies for the group. Don't be a lone ranger.

What should you look for in associate teachers? Spiritual maturity. Doctrinal purity. Regular attendance. Don't reward those who don't have time for you unless they are the teacher. Look for those who can prepare on short notice should you become suddenly ill or get called away. In short, look for someone you can trust, someone you can invest some time in as Paul invested in Timothy. Look for someone who can take your place. Constantly replicate yourself. It's the only way to be ready for the future.

This is not your Bible study; it belongs to God. He used you as a catalyst to get it going and to continue it. But should you be transferred to another state, should you take a leave of absence or even quit your job, that workplace Bible study should live on after you. That will be the case only if you prepare for it.

But there's more. I began this book by saying that the local church is God's ordained agency for evangelizing the world and equipping the saints. In teaching a Bible study, you are doing what God has called you to do in the workplace. What the Lord accomplishes through you in the lives of your colleagues is good, but it's not enough.

Steer group members to a Bible-teaching church

Every believer needs to be a part of a local church, worshiping corporately and serving faithfully. A key element in follow-up for your Bible study group is to see that each member is a fruitful member of a local, Bible-teaching church.

Since the church enjoys the primacy in God's plan for redeeming fallen mankind, your workplace Bible study must never become a substitute for His church. It is just an extension of your opportunity to be a servant of the Lord. You should steer every member of your study group into a local church.

"The Church is not a gallery for the exhibition of eminent Christians, but a school for the education of imperfect ones."
— Henry Ward Beecher

Recommending a specific church always carries with it some danger, so make your recommendation wisely. Begin with your church. If your local church is a place of genuine worship, praise, fellowship and service, suggest to your friends that they may enjoy attending where you are a member. If that's not possible, suggest they find a similar church in their neighborhood that you are familiar with.

Recommend only those churches that believe and teach that God's Word is accurate and inerrant, that Jesus is the divine Son of God and the only Savior of the world, and that faith in Christ is absolutely essential for salvation. There are other important issues, but any church that doesn't begin with these as givens isn't worthy of your recommendation.

The ultimate follow-up is done in the corporate experience of the local church. Don't fail to guide new believers to a church where Jesus would feel at home.

Be flexible and cooperative with your employer

The final follow-up is with your employer. You began by asking permission to have a workplace Bible study. That's being a responsible employee. But responsibility and common sense require that you keep your boss informed about what's going on in your group.

Tell your employer about your successes and victories. He or she may be more interested than you think. This will build a strong bridge to the future. Keeping your employer informed will help the group for years to come.

Sometimes your employer may need you to change the venue of your study group or even the time of your meeting. Be flexible and cooperative. If you are meeting in a company facility, this is all the more important. Pave the way for the future by being flexible in the present.

And by all means, stop your study on time. If you have one hour for lunch, do not come back late to work because you allowed your study to run over. Be disciplined. Follow-up with your employer is as important as follow-up with your group.

Conclusion

If you have the right view of work—that God gave it to you for good, that He gave it to you as a gift and that He gave it to you as a platform for service to Him—you will gain a new appreciation for how important a workplace Bible study can be. It's an extension of your church's outreach ministry through you. It's a natural, and since you spend a third of your life on the job, it's a way to integrate your faith with your vocation.

That may be a new concept for you, but it isn't for God. He never intended for us to divorce our work from our witness. It's only when we refuse to take the Bible to work that we lose one-third of our audience, one-third of our outreach and one-third of our opportunity to take the Gospel into all the world to every creature.

Think about it! You visit your mission field eight hours a day, every working day of your life. Why are you there if not as God's ambassador?

You *can* take your Bible to work. It's easier than you think. And the opportunities are greater than you imagine.

Back to the Bible is a nonprofit ministry dedicated to Bible teaching, evangelism and edification of Christians worldwide.

If we may assist you in knowing more about Christ and the Christian life, please write to us without obligation:

Back to the Bible
P.O. Box 82808
Lincoln, NE 68501